21st May 2005

Happy 60R Bir[...]
Love + [...]

The Ha[...]

C000108254

to Rosamug
on her 60ᵗ (!?)
best wishes
Norman

Happy Birthdays
from
Maxim

The Hare That Hides Within
Poems about St. Melangell

Edited by
Anne Cluysenaar and Norman Schwenk

PARTHIAN

Parthian
The Old Surgery
Napier Street
Cardigan
SA43 1ED
www.parthianbooks.co.uk

First published 2004

Reprinted 2004

Edited by Anne Cluysenaar and Norman Schwenk

ISBN 1-902638-38-7

Typeset in Sabon

Printed and bound by Dinefwr Press, Llandybïe

With Support from the Parthian Collective

Parthian is an independent publisher that works with the support of the
Arts Council of Wales and the Welsh Books Council

British Library Cataloguing in Publication Data
A cataloguing record for this book is available from the British Library

Cover Design: Richard Cox
Cover Illustration: Colin See-Paynton

CONTENTS

ACKNOWLEDGEMENTS

For her introduction Anne Cluysenaar acknowledges A.M. Allchin, *Pennant Melangell, Place of Pilgrimage*, Gwasg Santes Melangell, 1994.

The poems in this collection, if previously published, have appeared in the following publications and are printed with permission of the authors and editors:

Glenda Beagan 'Melangell' *Poetry Wales* and *Vixen* (Honno)

Ruth Bidgood 'Hare at Pennant' *Poetry Wales* and *The Fluent Moment* (Seren), 'Cwm Pennant' *Scintilla*

David Hart 'The Big Name' *New Welsh Review* and *Setting the Poem to Words* (Five Seasons Press)

Gwyneth Lewis 'Melangell Variations' *Scintilla*. This sequence was commissioned by the Swansea UK Year of Literature 1995.

Hilary Llewellyn-Williams 'The Innocent Hare' quotes John Crowley's novel *Little, Big*.

Norman Schwenk 'Ballad of St Melangell' (Alley Press poster). This poem quotes Samuel Taylor Coleridge's 'The Rime of the Ancient Mariner'.

FOREWORD

Just outside the entrance to the crypt chapel at Lambeth Palace is a wood carving of St Melangell (by Sister Bridget of Wantage); a bit of a puzzle to some visitors, but for many an object they want to touch and contemplate. It's a simple piece of work, a single solid bole of wood with Melangell's hare carved into her skirts, embraced by her hands, so that the whole is monumental and plain in its lines but full of fluid movement. It is all there – the forest, the urgency, the embrace, the holding of flight in stillness. It's a reminder of some of what makes the story of Melangell echo so strongly.

As Anne Cluysenaar says, and as many of the poems repeat, it is a story of fundamental conflicts, power and acquisition, the hunt, and refuge and peace, the praying woman. It dramatises the strength of contemplative resistance; it tells us that there is a place to be away from hunting. Whether this is read in connection with human abuse of nature, male abuse of women, or power's abuse of prayer in general, the pattern is similar. These poems build their own kind of shrine, like Pennant itself: a place to stand where you can resist whatever huntsman is in pursuit.

Rowan Williams
November, 2003

INTRODUCTION

It is impossible not to be surprised by the unique place in which St Melangell chose to settle. Ringed by hills, the narrow valley reaches towards what at first seems a dead end. As far as vehicles go, that is just what it is, but suddenly one catches sight of a long thin waterfall in the distance, whose brightness both closes off the valley and seems to open it to the sky. Near the road's end, the grey church occupies a circular bronze-age site. The present shape of the building dates from the fifteenth century, but a twelfth-century church and shrine preceded it, and in fact Pennant Melangell has been a place of pilgrimage and sanctuary for well over a thousand years.

The legend tells how Melangell, daughter of an Irish prince, found in this quiet valley a place in which she could follow her divine vocation. One day Prince Brochwel, to whom the land belonged, was hunting a hare. A seventeenth-century account tells how his hunting dogs pursued the hare to a thicket of brambles, full of thorns. In it he found a beautiful young woman praying. The hare was lying under the folds of her garment, fearlessly facing the dogs. Even so, the prince urged his hounds to attack, but they retreated howling. He then asked the woman how she had come to live on his land in such solitude. She said she had become aware that her father intended her to marry 'a great and generous Irishman' so, 'under the guidance of God', she had left her native land and come to Wales in order to live out instead a life of prayer and contemplation. She had not seen a human face for fifteen years. Prince Brochwel knew that God must have given refuge to the hare in recognition of this young woman's sincere and courageous faith. He did not hesitate now to call off his dogs. He also gave Melangell all the surrounding lands 'for the service of God', and as a sanctuary for 'any man or woman who has escaped here' on condition only that they in no way pollute the place. The legend tells that the saint lived in the valley for thirty-seven years. Her way of life was such that wild hares surrounded her as though they had been tame and, as the years went by, she attracted to Pennant Melangell women who wished to join her in a quiet and stable life of prayer.

In recent years, the legend of Saint Melangell has attracted increasing attention from poets in Wales. They have explored a range of different, even contrasting, meanings, revealing the complexity of what might seem at first hearing quite a straightforward tale. The hare is itself a beast of legend. Primarily seen as a creature of the Moon goddess, an emblem of fecundity and increase, it has also acquired many names. Most relevant to the poems in this collection are, perhaps: *the fast traveller, the way beater, the slink away, the one it's bad luck to meet, the dew-flirt, the wood-cat or puss.* Depending on which roles are taken to be primary, the significance of Melangell's protection, which is ultimately that of God, can be seen to shift. This very aspect of the legend is drawn to our attention by Ruth Bidgood when she imagines that the hare itself is aware of undergoing a change of character as it accepts sanctuary, surely a delicate emblem, this, for changes that may come to a human being able to feel himself or herself under divine protection. Prince Brochwel's decision not to continue the hunt but to provide a sanctuary not only for Melangell and for other human beings but also for wild beasts, has been interpreted as of ecological significance, an indication of the presence of the divine in all living things. Remembering the *Mabinogion,* R.S. Thomas wrote in 'The Minister' (1952):

> God is in the flowers
> Sprung at the feet of Olwen, and Melangell
> Felt his heart beating in the wild hare.

In some of these poems there is also recognition of a sexual element in the confrontation between a powerful prince and a solitary virgin. We are led to recognise the overwhelming nature of an experience which could hold such a man back, not only from hunting legitimate quarry but also from violating an unknown woman's sanctuary of thorns. In this interpretation it is as though the hare, symbol of fertility both natural and sacred, has become an emblem of the most intimate aspects of human existence and survival.

Since the earliest days of human prehistory, certain places have been valued as 'threshholds' over which the imagination may step towards deeper realities than the everyday. Pennant Melangell is such a place. Even to the saint herself, it must have seemed already ancient. Perhaps she would have recognised traces of prior occupation. Certainly the great yew tree near the church must have been some six hundred years old when she sat beneath it. She would have been aware of lasting things and short-lived things, and of her own place among them. No matter what the visitor's spiritual perspective, Pennant Melangell is full of resonances. While visible forms may alter over time, anyone visiting the place will still be aware of a threshhold tension, a sense of now and forever.

Saint Melangell's shrine is of a kind we hardly ever see elsewhere. Most such shrines, if they survived the middle ages, were destroyed at the Reformation. Saint Melangell's shrine was indeed broken up but sensitively rebuilt in the early 1990's, using as guides fragments of the original structure. The nave and chancel are separated by a beautifully carved fifteenth-century Rood Screen depicting the legend in impressively simple terms. The carving of the legend is underlined by a frieze of oak-leaves; at one end, significantly, we see a Green Man, oak-leaves spilling from his mouth; at the other, a hand holding a vine, perhaps, as A.M. Allchin remarks, a symbol of the creative power at work in nature.

For centuries the legend of Melangell, and Pennant Melangell itself as a numinous threshold, have stimulated poets to write in both the languages of Wales. More recently, in Allchin's words, 'among Welsh writers who work in English, Melangell has been evoking new and original responses'.

It is now ten years since the shrine was restored and became again a year-round centre for pilgrimage and healing. This collection of modern poems inspired by Saint Melangell is published in celebration of the continuing impact of both the place and the legend on the poetic imagination of Wales.

Anne Cluysenaar
August, 2003

God is in the flowers
Sprung at the feet of Olwen, and Melangell
Felt his heart beating in the wild hare.

from R.S.Thomas 'The Minister'

GLENDA BEAGAN

MELANGELL

They call me saint.
They bless me and the hares they call my lambs,
here, in quietness of forest, fastness
of mountain wall.

Pennant is my place,
mellow paps the hills behind my home,
dappled cones sunlight plays upon,
with clouds dancing.

Fierce beasts were the waves
that tossed me, my landfall so
far west of here. Through winter's mire and frost
I struggled.

A carlin, hooped
in age gave me bowed wisdom, broth
in a dish of bone, simples and salves.
The body mends at last.

The spirit grows
to a glade's calm, chill of well water,
bannocks of coarse flour. I delve and hew,
Erin remembering.

Tanat rejoicing.
Then comes the summer of mallows and wild lupins
blue as streams on soft banks of seed,
the cry of the hunt,

the blare and wild
will of hounds, till through birches they come like a fire
running, a hare at my hem, a huntsman's horn singed
to his lips in a blister of sound.

They call it miracle,
and so it was, I, frozen in his prince's sight, never
having seen a man so like a god, a flame. His name is
                                                    Brochwel
and I, a bride of Christ...

My hares, my lambs
are sweet velvet nutmegs. I have seen them dancing
in moonlight. At the *prie dieu* I leave posies
of white broom.

Maidens flock here,
craving this rule, this life I blend. As years
mount the arch of the sky, I kneel and whisper,
plaiting staunch cords of peace.

RUTH BIDGOOD

HARE AT PENNANT

I Hare have been the clever one,
up to my tricks, always a winner,
fooling man and beast – but not now,
not you, pretty lady, holy one.
You untwist my deviousness.
I huddle at your feet
in your garments' folds,
and am simple hare, fool hare, hunted hare.
I have doubled and doubled,
am spent, blown, not a trick left
to baffle pursuers.
A leap of despair
has brought me to you.

Cudd fi, Melangell,
Monacella, hide me!

*

'Seize him!' I cried to my hounds
(the best, I had thought, in all
my princedom of Powys).
But each time I chivvied them on,
the fools came squealing and squelking back.
So I rode into tanglewood,
my huntsmen after me,
the wretched scruff-hounds skulking off;
and she was there in the glade,
still as an image, still
as her carved Christ on his cross.

I pictured her alone with me;
but this was no girl from the huts
to be gripped and thrown aside
for a paltry coin, no absent warrior's
hungry wife. Cool as moonlight
this maiden waited on wet grass,
looking up at me with no fear, no blame,
and by her small bare feet,
panting and peeping, crouched the hare.

I saw how it would be; she'd get her land
from me, the prayer-girl, to make
a sanctuary here – and Powys
would go short of hare-meat
and the dark strong broth! I
would make my peace with the cringing dogs,
hunt forests to the north for other prey,
yet leave a thought behind me here
for her to shelter.

Cudd fi, Melangell,
Monacella, hide me!

*

Once I was Great Hare
and the Moon's companion,
and Easter's acolyte bearing the light.
Victim, I ran charred through heath-fire,
lay bloodied in last corn.
I was warped to hold the soul of a witch:
dwindled to trickster and buffoon.
Men dodge my real, unchancy name,
calling me cat-shanks, cabbager,

dew-fellow, cat-of-the-furze,
maze-maker, leaper-to-hill.
False, broken is my boast of winning;
I crouch in dread of the fangs.
All I have been, am, she shelters.
 'Not I', she says, 'it is my Lord'. But she
is what I know, soft-robed saint,
gentle one, who heard my piping cry,

Cudd fi, cudd fi, Melangell,
Monacella, hide me!

CWM PENNANT

1 Patron Saint

Within the girdle of her care she keeps
the farms of her narrow valley. Far upstream
one house is new, foursquare, boldly red,
others insubstantial grey
across fields, at the foot of hills.
A stranger on the road has to peer
to catch the dark of windows without glass.

Within the girdle of her care she keeps her church,
its ancient round of holy land
under hanging woods, in sight
of wilder heights beyond;
its intricate gnarl, dark spread of yews
over tip-tilt slabs of lettered stone.
At her May festival one bell sounds.
Her people have got up early, and press in
to pray, generation on generation
with never a jostle, while small warm rain
gentles their waiting homes.

2 Iorwerth Drwyndwn

They say that he, Iorwerth the blemished one,
had a refuge here, where Dafydd his brother
killed him for the lands of Arfon.

They say that if
by conquest and the death of brothers
Iorwerth had lorded it over all
their father's lands, he could not inherit
(lop-nosed from youth) the name of King.

They say that men
still held the old, merciless
dogma – marred King, weak realm;
would not have much lamented
this death in the secret valley, being used
to culling blemished beasts.

They say that all,
kneeling by taper-light at the shrine,
would own themselves blemished,
their inheritance bought back for them
by mercy; would then go out shriven, and meet
again the ancient inexorable dark.

3 Legends of Giants

In these mountains are legends of giants;
Balaam, Owty, Rhuddwen, Myfyr.
Some were nameless, like the jumping giant
of Moel Dinmoel, who left a well
where he landed. Not gods,
not angels, they were vulnerable
in their disproportion, not at home
amid hills meant to be looked up to,
paradigms of grandeur and mystery –
but to them, footstools, springboards, offering
nothing bigger than themselves. Lumpy,
passionate, destructive, the giants lumbered
through the landscape, here and there
casually altering it with dropped loads
of enormous rocks, springs bursting out
where great heels crushed the hill.

One huge guilt-ridden creature –
outlawed maybe, slayer of his kin? –
came crashing to Cwm Pennant by cockcrow,
seeking sanctuary at Melangell's church,
where the scale of power had a different measure;
where he could be small, comforted,
and die, perhaps, into the innocence
he had always been blundering towards.

4 Saint Melangell and the Green Man

High on the roodscreen, the Saint's legend
has pride of place. In pleated robe
she stands between huntsman and hare;
the dogs will never catch it.
But the crozier she holds came later.
She was a hermit first, for years,
sleeping on a rock in the wildwood;
all round her, matings and deaths
in the fecund, perilous night.

The screen is carved with branches of oak,
plumply-fashioned acorns, that mean life,
completeness. It would be easy to miss
in a corner above the pulpit
the Green Man, wild leafy face,
huge eyes desperate to comprehend
what will be.
                    The King of the Oak must die.
Pilgrim, pray for lovers: virgin,
with your verities, cherish deciduous joy.

ANNE CLUYSENAAR

ON A VISIT TO PENNANT MELANGELL

1

As we catch sight
they become secrets.

Leaf opened out
into wings, their dark
absorbed by light-flow,
up-stream, down-stream?

A squiggle, from lichen
to the tightness of grass-blades,
far off now or propped
close by, on spread paws?

She would have known.
Here, the dipper.
Here, the lizard.
In their usual places.

2

In this Welsh valley
her Irish Gaelic
quested for God.
The valley speaks
no language. In exile
she was at home,
trusting the place.

ANNE CLUYSENAAR

A tightness of hills.
Shale with mudstone
or greenly wooded.
The cwm closed
by a fall of water,
a streak shining,
distant, still.

She saw it all.
Sat under this yew,
hundreds of years
heavy in its branches.
The bark flaking.
Hollow at the centre
where the shoot grows.

3

Hounds on the hills.
The hunters' hooves.
A horn halooing.

She knelt among thorns.
At her hem, the hare
crouched down, breathless.

Her prayer has made
a strangeness in the shadows,
a houseless threshold.

In the sun, outside,
hounds whimper, doubting,
steeds stretch their necks.

The prince dismounts.
Hesitates. Alone.
Fate is upon him.

4

We notice in the fields
thorns that were hedges.
Their broken lines
mark changing borders.

What will let us in?
What will keep us out?
The bounds are new.
Our time confronts us.

5

We're among surfaces.
Signs that say 'Private'.
Cards to be bought.
A visitors book.
Strangers smiling.

Round this bronze-age site
a circular wall.
Five yellow poppies.
I cup one. My palm
holds a splash of light.

Lean on the yew.
Not only the lizard,
the dipper, the hare
hiding in the open.
It's all here, hiding.

JOHN FREEMAN

THE REBIRTH OF BROCHWEL

Because I hunted the hare
I found this holy maid.
She disciplined my desire:
the hare was not to be seized.

Over my anger stole
a sweetness of a kind
I had not hoped to taste,
from the love in her mind.

Some pain in me dissolved,
and the dissolving itself
was painful. Began to dissolve.
An old unconscious grief.

I, Brochwel the Fanged, Prince
of Powys, who was a god,
became a happier thing,
man at last, again child.

For twenty-two years I had been
alone, trusting nobody
completely, knowing the world.
Never until this day.

Loving only so much
as I could afford to love
in the knowledge that no
devotion I ever gave

was ever merited,
or ever fully returned.
Outwardly always obeyed,
but truly at heart spurned.

When the lady of the hare
spoke, the whole deep vale
in which we stood brimmed
with something that made me whole.

The hare I had hunted gazed
from the lady's folded skirts.
For the first time I saw
what I had wanted to hurt:

the beautiful long ears,
the fur, gentle eyes.
Tenderness flooded me
and left me gasping, dazed.

Lady and hare were one,
an emblem of true power,
the power to love and heal,
not the false power of war.

The voice of the human part
and the animal's soft gaze
were the means by which this
single vision gave peace.

Hunting is soldiering. I had gone
as if armoured, as if
holding a heavy sword.
The wave of love and relief

that swept over me made
the imagined armour and sword
fall off me like a mask.
I was new-made, restored.

To lady and hare I gave
as their sanctuary part
of my princely lands. No
person should do them hurt.

My strong arms would protect
this greater strength evermore.
Now in proud humility,
I ask pilgrims to hear:

pray to this saint, revere
her defenceless emblem, the hare.
But remember I too
am joined to this holy pair.

Without my energy, first
destructive, then made well
by her as a great shield,
there would have been no tale,

no legend, no sanctuary.
Come you like me, then, here
to give your discordant life
to Melangell to make clear.

You need her healing love.
She will flourish from the good
you take from here to do
in her name in the world.

MARION GLASSCOE

VISITATIONS

Last night, climbing to the ridge of the hill,
I suddenly met you, head-on, loping
peacefully up the other side, coming
straight on at me as if I was not there.
I held my dog still. We stood enthralled.
Your russet fur was tipped with summer's fire
in the last of the sun; your wide-set eyes,
pale lamps, angle-poised, raked behind you,
side-tracking the shadows – guarding your back.
If I had not called at the last minute
you would have gambolled straight into our legs.
As it was, you paused.
Yellow eyes flickered into our gaze,
holding us, motionless, before you
bowed amiably, then veered away, swift
down the uncut field, your great launching pads
bobbing like pollened tufts of vernal grass,
leaving us standing.

Was it like this
with Melangell? I guess it would have been
hunting season, after the corn was cut
and the first frosts come, when, one rimed morning,
careless, you bounded out of silence
under snow-tipped hills into the orbit
of a maelstrom of hounds and the taunting
clarion of a horn that hurt your long ears.
On the instant you changed gear and fled
like the wind funnelling up the valley,

your sights set behind you on the proud man
and his designer dogs. Did you not see
the girl coming from under yew trees
until you hit her legs running? Tangled,
trembling, under her skirts, were you aware
of clamorous tongues toned down to whining fear
and that insistent horn abruptly silenced?
Did you emerge at last to find only
the freshness of morning, and a girl,
newly possessed of sanctuary,
laughing quietly to herself at this
apparent serendipity of grace?

DAVID HART

THE BIG NAME

In the little house
of the big name
(in the valley
with the buzzards
and the sheep),

at the altar of
the little house
of the big name
(in the clearing
with the graves
of the poor who stayed),

in the regular singing
at the altar
of the little house
of the big name
(where the yew trees
predate the big name's son

when he was on our planet
speaking
in the big name's name),
I can't forget
my own
but clothe it
with stone.

GRAHAM HARTILL

BROCHWEL LOOKS BACK ON MELANGELL

I felt like a bird that stooped to the hare in me.
All my life I'd been told to trample the womanly thing,
our game being power and heavy skill,
but when I fell, my sins
flew off from me like flies from cess
and I didn't know where to put my eyes,
that little animal trembling under her skirt!
She looked like a hedgehog, an urchin run off from an
                                            orphanage,
some baggage on the loose, with hair hung down like
                                            scruffy willow.
   'So what do you really want to see?' she said.
I spat and tossed my hat off, but she didn't move
(the little animal bucking beneath her skirt).
Her eyes were waving grey and black, like poplar trees
                                            in wind
and I was pinned by them, thrown back against my scorn.
Oh yes, she knew I could have captured more than
                                            just a hare!
But I just stood.

   And that's what got to me: a falcon
tumbling to a prey I suddenly didn't recognise,
   I sheered off.

That hare was like a little Christ sent skipping to his
                                            mother's thighs.

*

Look, I must do something more
than merely tell you this. The words
are just too plain, not plain enough!

You poets know it:
words are little gods to you.

I've tried to hunt the word with enough of God in it
to do her right.

And when I'm dead, please pin a little scratch of skin
of me to Peter's door.

It seems like all my life's been battering it.

*

Since Melangell
I've set the dogs on men
and forced a girl or two, like soldiers do
(Well poets? what do you expect?)
But lying down with her would be a softer, sadder thing:

her skull so velvety and scarred,

her breast a tent for all my violent griefs,

my sins descending on us through the night
like bright and ceaseless rain.

GWYNETH LEWIS

MELANGELL VARIATIONS

1 The Story

Not that the hunting wasn't hard that day –
the greyhounds running whole rivers of scents –
not that we'd let much get away
not that the hare wasn't innocent

but canny as we ran her to ground
into a thicket. Not that she cried
more than they do...but that she found
a girl in a thornbush and tried to hide

herself in her petticoats, sun under cloud.
She sat there, a letter, the start of a tome
about stillness. The master allowed
the dogs to calm down. They settled, at home

watching the virgin in her shaking tree.
Her silence made the cool glade burn.
The seeker's found. Melangell, teach me,
the hunter you coursed and caught, where to turn.

2 Her Silence

Breathe in.
She's quiet as a mist on moss.
Breathe out,
subtle as a burning bog.

Breathe in...
The sea sighs as she holds quite still
...and out
storms ride on her breath, a gale

of nothing. *Breathe in.*
Words fall in a drop from a thorn...
Breathe out.
...earth hums its tone as planets turn

around her. *Breathe in.*
Her gravity holds us. Hush. Her thought
gives us a world – *breathe out* –
where insects move like juggernauts.

Breathe in. We swim
to drown, Melangell, in your breath
which drags us from our land-bound doubt
towards you. *Out...Breathe out...Breathe out...*

3 Prayer For Modern Times

You're built for transport. Our Lady of the Traffic Cones
give us this day our dose of speed

along the bypass. Let us not change gear
too often. Let us have free will

of roundabouts, not traffic-light
predestination. Make the town lamps blur

as we pass, in stereo rock n' roll.
You are our sliproad to the motorway

away from being dull. You are
our cats' eyes in the dark of here.

Eidetic image of a passing car.
The double sun of headlights flare

before the crash that keeps us all intact,
wheels spinning on a petrol-bleeding track.

4 The Tropic Zone

The rain, in skirts, has covered the hill
and hidden the hare of the sun in cloud.
Under the trees the fern flames lick
at tree trunks. She is with us now,

under vines engorged with dark and damp.
Orchids open their pouting lips
as stones cry out and speak of bread.
A flash of colour – a parakeet

breaks through the sun-gold canopy.
In her all umbrellas turn parasols,
the oak a palm tree in the tropic zone
her virtue's translated. The gibbons call

our souls to their exotic selves –
at home, but different – and the roar
of her ethereal lions makes the aloes bloom
rare, but familiar where no fears are.

5 Atomic Saint

Look through her.
For Melangell is a door.

Fall with her –
stone through clearest pool
of coldest water.

She is motes of dust in air,
impediment that shows the light
in all its wholeness.

She is a living flame. Her hair
has lit up cities.
It is herself she burns. She has
a half-life of ten thousand years
and then grows hotter.

She is a pestilence.
Her soul's bright spores
have slaughtered thousands who have lived
in her virtue's gardens.

This is the death we've all been living for.

6 A Cloud of Witnesses

Melangell, in your box of lead,
find us.

Brynach, Beuno, Tudno, Llyr.

The earth's your sleeping hare, will jump
to greet you.

Tysul, Teilo, Gwynlliw...Rain

will rub its pelt of weather hard
against blind windscreens...

Padarn, Maelog, Gwendolen...
until we feel the mountains move

towards you, Twrog, Rhystud, Llawen, Gwaur.
In company, the light grows great
around you – headlamps shine across the dark

from Cadfan, Rhydian, Sannan teg
and through the gloom of space we see
the sun take shelter in your spirit's sky
and you surrounded by the daylight stars
of other saints who shall not die –
Cynog, Padarn, Edeyrn Fawr.

From time, our hunter, guard us with your prayer
Melangell, strongest steel and softest air.

HILARY LLEWELLYN-WILLIAMS

THE INNOCENT HARE

Poor Puss is running with the dogs
in the sunrise all thick with May dew
poor Puss with her heart clamouring
blood pumping the long muscles of her thighs

her eyes staring behind at death
hot on her trail with yelps and yammering
her eyes full of green and hawthorn
open to each spark and flutter of life

All last night she grazed on the mountain
moonlight silvering her closecropped fur
all last night she leapt in the grasses
creeping at dawn to her shallow and thorny set

But the hunt is up and she is bounding
over the scree and down to the valley
the hunt is up and she steers and weaves
through bog and bracken guided by Tanat's stream

following the cool voice of water
rinsing her throat with dappled promises
following the damp smell of cresses
teasing her ears with secrets and shadowing

So when the hunter comes to the quiet place
his dogs fled scattered and searching
when the hunter comes to the holy well
all he sees is a young woman kneeling

innocent and dressed in plain grey
her hood thrown over her and slender hands
innocently upraised to praise the day
O great wide wonderful beautiful world she prays

Some say the hare is hid beneath my apron
the bonny hare crouched there
under my skirts she smiles and whoever dares
to lift my shining veil will be struck to stone

Honey-gold the grove in sunlight
where the hunter stands entranced
by the honey-gold of her hair
and by the curling waters in the pool

Sweet Puss is flown and gone
underneath and hidden from our eyes
sweet Puss is lying low in the hollows
of the earth all dressed for the pilgrimage of spring

NORMAN SCHWENK

RIME OF ST MELANGELL

We celebrate the risen church
Of Melangell the Fair,
Our gentle, fierce and loving saint
Who guards the hunted hare.

She halts the red-eyed, running dogs
With one dismissive frown.
They scent the hare but do not dare
To rend this lady's gown.

They mill around, poor sheepish hounds,
Lap at the laughing brook,
Then find some fascinating smell
To shun her dreaded look

And lope back to their kennels warm.
The furious hunter grips
His horn and finds it frozen fast
Onto his puckered lips.

'Who are you, lovely virgin witch?'
He cries when he can speak.
'Why charm my hounds and hunting horn?
Why spoil our hide-and-seek?'

'I am from far North,' she replies –
Her black eyes hold him tight –
'And weary of running, like the hare,
Hounded day and night,

Because I dared to spurn a man
My father bade me wed.
I chose another man myself
And took him to my bed.

Now he is dead and I am fled,
A homeless, hunted waif,
And when I found this hidden vale
I prayed I might be safe.'

'I am a Welsh prince. Safe you are.
This land is mine by right.'
He tells himself he loves the witch,
But what he feels is fright.

'This land belongs to God,' she whispers.
'All his creatures share.
Beware the sin of Pride,' she says.
'Be humble like the hare.'

'There are too many of the beasts!
They breed like flies in dung!'
He dares glance in her eyes again
And sees his body hung

Feet upwards from a blackened yew
Like so much strangled game.
He loves this lady: waves of terror
Flutter through his frame.

And then she lifts her muddied gown.
The hare from under creeps
To run and play another day.
And then the tall prince weeps.

And ever since this hidden vale
Has been her church and home.
And pilgrims have long ages come
For healing prayer and song.

One time the Men of Reason came,
Covered with blood and gore.
They broke her shrine, scattered her bones,
Unchained the Dogs of War.

But now her place is whole again,
And pilgrims line the ways,
And experts come from far and near
To denigrate or praise.

We celebrate Saint Melangell
And bless her in our time.
We love the hare that hides within
And sing the ancient rhyme:

'He prayeth best, who loveth best
All things both great and small;
For the dear God who loveth us,
He made and loveth all'.

BIOGRAPHICAL NOTES

Glenda Beagan is a native of Rhuddlan, where she still lives. As a mature student she gained a First Class Honours in English at University College, Aberystwyth, followed by an M.A. in Creative Writing at the University of Lancaster. She has published two volumes of short stories *The Medlar Tree* and *Changes and Dreams* (Seren) and a collection of poems *Vixen* (Honno).

Ruth Bidgood was born in Seven Sisters (Blaendulais) Glamorgan. After many years away from Wales she returned in the 1960s and now lives in mid-Wales, where all her books have been written. A *New and Selected Poems* is due from Seren in 2004. Three of her books have won Arts Council of Wales awards. She is also the author of a prose book, *Parishes of the Buzzard*, about the Abergwesyn area of North Breconshire (Alun Books) and articles about local history in county journals.

Anne Cluysenaar was born in Belgium, finished her schooling in Ireland, received a degree from Trinity College, Dublin, and in the sixties took Irish citizenship. She now lives on a smallholding in Wales. Her selected poems *Timeslips* (Carcanet) contains a sequence 'Vaughan Variations', exploring themes from the work of the Breconshire poet Henry Vaughan. She edits poetry for *Scintilla*, the yearly journal of the Usk Valley Vaughan Association. Forthcoming publications include *Henry Vaughan: Selected Poems* (SPCK) and a new collection containing autobiographical lyrics together with narrative meditations on the life and work of the great Usk-born naturalist Alfred Russel Wallace.

John Freeman teaches English Literature at Cardiff University, where he also taught Creative Writing for many years. His poetry has been widely published in magazines and anthologies. Collections include *The Light Is Of Love, I Think: New and Selected Poems* (Stride) and *Landscape and Portraits* (Redbeck Press). He has also published a book of essays *The Less Received: Neglected Modern Poets* (Stride), articles on George Eliot and Shelley, and has edited *Beats, Bohemians and Intellectuals* by Jim Burns (Trent Editions).

Marion Glasscoe graduated in English from the Universities of Edinburgh and London and lectured on Medieval Literature and Art at Exeter University. She has published widely in this field, particularly on contemplative writers, and remains a General Editor for Exeter Medieval Texts and Studies (Exeter University Press). She has a smallholding in mid-Devon and is relishing the opportunity to write poetry in her retirement.

David Hart was born and grew up in Aberystwyth and now lives in Birmingham where he works as a freelance writer and poet. He has formerly been an Anglican university chaplain, a theatre critic and an arts administrator. He has won major poetry prizes and held several writers' residencies. He is currently Writer in Residence at Heartlands General Hospital, Birmingham, and an Honorary Teaching Fellow at the University of Warwick. Books of poems include *Setting the Poem to Words* and a poem in response to Bardsey Island *Crag Inspector*, both Five Seasons Press.

Graham Hartill is currently working as a facilitator with the Ledbury Poetry Festival. His book of transcription poems from the Festival, *Lifelines*, was published in 2003. Apart from several of his own collections, Graham has written translations and adaptations from the Chinese. He is a contributor to Parthian's anthology *The Pterodactyl's Wing: Welsh World Poetry. Cennau's Bell*, his selected poems, is out soon from the Collective Press. He lives with his family in the Black Mountains of southern Wales.

Gwyneth Lewis writes in both Welsh, her first language, and in English. She has published five collections of poetry in both languages, and her latest book in Welsh *Y Llofrudd Iaith (The Language Murderer)* won the Arts Council of Wales Book of the Year prize. She was recently awarded a five-year fellowship from the National Endowment for Science, Technology and the Arts, and is currently writing a book based on her experiences sailing to foreign ports associated with Cardiff in its heyday. Her latest book in English is *Keeping Mum* from Bloodaxe.

Hilary Llewellyn-Williams lived in West Wales for many years and now lives in Pontypool. Seren has published four collections of her poetry, the latest *Greenland*. She has read her work in Britain, Spain, New Zealand and Portugal, and has recently been collaborating with the composer Ian Lawson on a musical setting of her sequence *The Tree Calendar*. She has tutored for the Arvon Foundation and Ty Newydd, and until recently taught Literature and Creative Writing at Cardiff University. She now teaches at the University of Glamorgan.

Norman Schwenk was until his retirement Convenor of Creative Writing at Cardiff University. He now works as a freelance writer and teacher. He has two collections of verse in print, *The Black Goddess* (Chiron Press) and *How To Pronounce Welsh Place Names* (Alley Press), and another forthcoming *The More Deceived: Poems About Love and Lovers*. He is currently working on a collection of short stories *My Dog Can Talk*. American by birth, he has lived in Wales since the 1960s.